Maths Around Us

Patterns at the Museum

Tracey Steffora

www.raintreepublishers.co.uk
Visit our website to find out more information about Raintree books.

To order:

☎ Phone 0845 6044371

🖷 Fax +44 (0) 1865 312263

🖳 Email myorders@raintreepublishers.co.uk

Customers from outside the UK please telephone +44 1865 312262

Raintree is an imprint of Capstone Global Library Limited, a company incorporated in England and Wales having its registered office at 7 Pilgrim Street, London, EC4V 6LB – Registered company number: 6695582

Edited by Rebecca Rissman, Tracey Steffora, and Catherine Veitch
Designed by Joanna Hinton-Malivoire
Picture research by Elizabeth Alexander
Production by Victoria Fitzgerald
Originated by Capstone Global Library Ltd
Printed and bound in China by Leo Paper Products Ltd

ISBN 978 1 406 22316 3 (hardback)
15 14 13 12 11
10 9 8 7 6 5 4 3 2 1

ISBN 978 1 406 22324 8 (paperback)
16 15 14 13 12
10 9 8 7 6 5 4 3 2 1

British Library Cataloguing in Publication Data
Steffora, Tracey.
Patterns at the museum. -- (Maths around us)
516.1'5-dc22

Acknowledgements
The author and publisher are grateful to the following for permission to reproduce photographs: Alamy pp. 5 (© Martin Thomas Photography), 6 (© Rolf Adlercreutz), 7 (© First Light), 8 (© David Rowland), 9 (© eddie linssen), 10 (© imagebroker), 13 (© Joe Vogan), 15 (© Oliver Knight), 17 (© Finnbarr Webster), 20 (© Urbanmyth), 21 right (© Urbanmyth), 21 left (© Urbanmyth), 21 middle (© World Pictures), 22 (© dave Jepson), 23 glossary – armour (© eddie linssen), 23 glossary – bone (© Oliver Knight), 23 glossary – tile (© Finnbarr Webster); Corbis pp. 4 (© Emely), 11 (© Steven Vidler/Eurasia Press), 19 (© Dan Forer/Beateworks).

Cover photograph of a spiral staircase in the Vatican Museum, Vatican City, Rome reproduced with permission of Alamy (© First Light). Back cover photograph of colourful shutters reproduced with permission of Alamy (© imagebroker).

We would like to thank Nancy Harris, Dee Reid, and Diana Bentley for their assistance in the preparation of this book.

Every effort has been made to contact copyright holders of material reproduced in this book. Any omissions will be rectified in subsequent printings if notice is given to the publisher.

Contents

At the museum

Look around the museum.

Patterns are everywhere.

Lines

Lines can make a pattern.

The lines on these stairs make
a pattern.

Shapes

Shapes can make a pattern.

The shapes on this armour make
a pattern.

Colours

Colours can make a pattern.

The colours on this boat make
a pattern.

Find the pattern

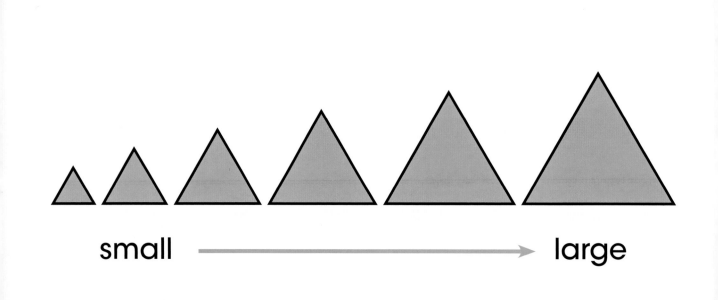

small ⟶ large

A pattern can go from small to large.

Can you see a pattern in these tiles?

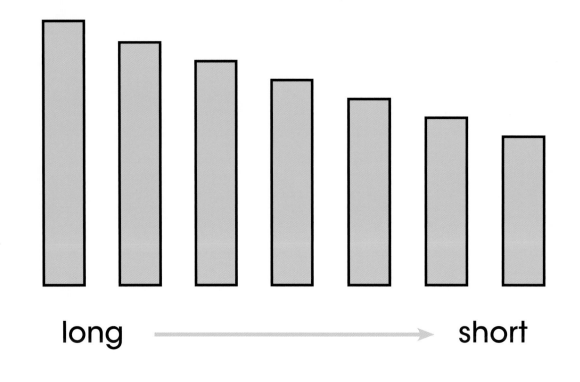

long ———————————→ short

A pattern can go from long to short.

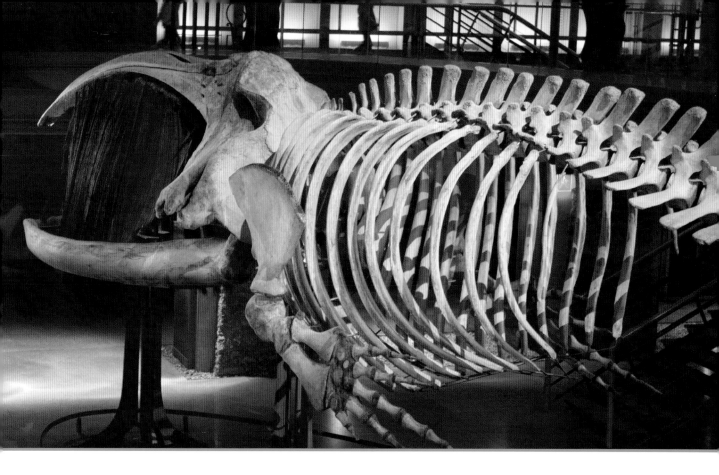

Can you see a pattern in these bones?

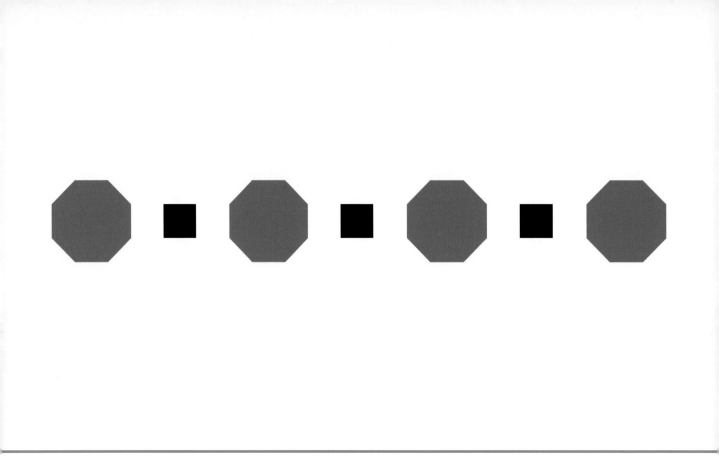

A pattern can repeat.

Can you see a pattern on this floor?

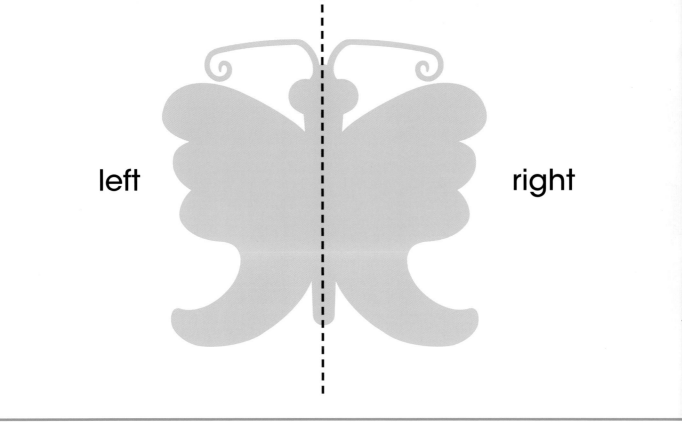

left   right

A pattern can match on the left and the right.

Can you see a pattern with these lions?

Look for a pattern in these windows.

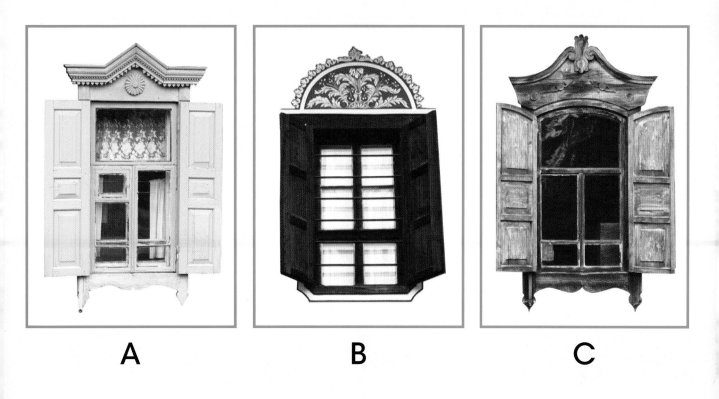

A   B   C

Which one comes next?

21

How many patterns can you find?

Picture glossary

 **armour** metal covering that protects the body in battle

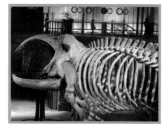 **bone** part of the body that forms the skeleton

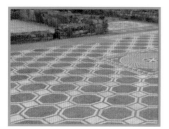 **tile** piece of material used to cover floors or walls

Index

Notes for parents and teachers

Before reading

When observing patterns, children are dealing with objects that have a relationship to each other. They are required to respond in a logical way to what they see. Provide children with sets of objects (blocks, beads, coins, leaves) and encourage them to order the objects in different ways (e.g. biggest to smallest, smallest to biggest). Discuss how putting things in order is a type of pattern.

After reading

Review the different types of patterns found in the text. With children, go on a pattern hunt in your school or local environment. Take along a digital camera to record what you find. Print out the photos and sort them with children (e.g., patterns that use lines, colours, shapes). You might then choose to use them in constructing a book.